UNSPOKEN WORDS

ALEXANDER R. STEWART

UNSPOKEN WORDS

THE THOUGHTS OF A SOLDIER

PALMETTO
PUBLISHING
Charleston, SC
www.PalmettoPublishing.com

Copyright © 2023 by Alexander R. Stewart

All rights reserved

No portion of this book may be reproduced, stored in a retrieval system, or transmitted in any form by any means–electronic, mechanical, photocopy, recording, or other–except for brief quotations in printed reviews, without prior permission of the author.

Paperback ISBN: 979-8-8229-3923-3
eBook ISBN: 979-8-8229-3924-0

I would like to dedicate this book to all of the military men and women who have served their country. There are no words that could ever come close to repaying you and your families for your bravery and sacrifice.
—*Alexander R. Stewart*

Table of Contents

Sandy Boots. 1
Alarm. 2
"P.T.S.D.". 5
The Soldier Marches On. 7
Take a Life. 9
WE FIGHT!. 11
The Flag 13
Good Ole Jodi. 15
The Soldier's Resolve. 17
The Count Down 19
Sitting Alone. 20
Fireworks. 23
Intrusive Thoughts (Unwanted Guest) 25
"The Letter". 27
The Sentry. 29
Take a Knee. 31
Behavioral Health 33
Incoming, Incoming, Incoming! 35
Why We Drink 37
Broken Switch. 39
About the Author 41

Sandy Boots

A hard way of living,
yeah, that's what I've got.
If you slack off, or you slip up,
then you end up getting shot.
The training it is hard,
the deployments, they are worse.
The things you see and go through make the smoothest souls coarse.
So, if I come off sort of rough, I'm not trying to be rude.
I'm just another Soldier with some sand on their boots.

Alarm

They've raised the alarm.

I reach for my gear.
Stumbling, racing, ignoring my fear.
I throw my armor up onto my back
While another voice screams, "We are under attack!"

I start to run, rushing toward my door,
But then a loud noise throws me onto the floor.
What is this ringing, and pain in my head?
I cannot stand up, paralyzed as the dead.

A hand reaches out, I'm dragged cross the floor.
The hand guiding me safely up out of my door.
Another loud noise, and a large blinding light
Takes the hand guiding me out of my sight.

I hear my Sergeant take count of our heads,
It is then that I see that my best friend is dead.
He lies on the ground filthy, covered in blood
His image misty, blurry, like water stirred up with mud.

My friend was the hand guiding me out of my door,
My friend who just saved me, now lies dead on the floor.
My eyes fill with tears as I scream out his name
Wanting reply, which of course never came.

I watched as they loaded him onto that bird,
And out of me uttered, not one single word.
We pack up his things, his letters and gear,
Heads hanging low knowing he is not here.

The battle is over and we must go on,
Forever knowing that our friend is now gone.
With a heavy heart, I lay back down my head,
And with all of my might, try to go back to bed.

……They've raised the alarm.

"P.T.S.D."

P is for *Pain*.
In the memories that stay,
the wounds that they gave, and the scars that won't fade.
In the sting of a bullet, or the loss of a friend,
and the thoughts of a face that you won't see again.

T is for *Terror*.
Forever living on edge,
with worries and thoughts it will happen again.
Whether still overseas, or back in your home,
the feeling creeps up whenever you are alone.

S is for *Sickness*.
For which there is no cure,
for the thoughts and the feelings you just have to endure.
From the knots in your stomach, to the thoughts in your head
that sometimes make you think you are better off dead.

D is for *Dismay*.
The hopeless feeling you get,
when you think of the past, and the things you regret.
That hole you fall into, with these thoughts from your head,
and sometimes it feels you can't climb out again.

This is my new war, though I know you can't see,
as I fight for my life against *PTSD*.

The Soldier Marches On

Stepping timely to the drum, the Soldier marches on.
A thousand miles away from home, the Soldier marches on.

Although he's tired and wants to rest, the Soldier marches on.
Giving each task his very best, the Soldier marches on.

Through the fights that last him far too long, the Soldier marches on.
Though tomorrow he knows he may be gone, the Soldier marches on.

Through the blood, the pain, the agony, the Soldier marches on.
Although friend's deaths are saddening, the Soldier marches on.

For his family, his country, and his home, the Soldier marches on.
For he knows he never stands alone, the Soldier marches on.

Take a Life

Do you think you could do it, the same as I've done,
Do what it takes so the battle is won?
The task it is quick, not physically tough,
but it may just as well leave your mind feeling rough.
No; it's not a person, father, husband, or son.
We tell ourselves lies just to get the job done.

With a pull of the trigger the muzzle goes flash,
releasing the carbon, ejecting the brass.
As the round hits its target, dropping them to the ground,
I can still hear their screams as their blood spills around.
Final moments of terror, of pain, and regret,
the faces they made I will never forget.

Their voices and faces branded onto my brain,
reliving these moments 'til they drive me insane.
Though the battle is over, and the day it is won,
a battle within you has just barely begun.
These memories they haunt me as I lay down at night,
so I ask could you do it, could you take a life?

WE FIGHT!

WE FIGHT!
Thousands of miles from home,
WE FIGHT!
Though we miss our families,
WE FIGHT!
Although we may not feel wanted,
WE FIGHT!
Although we're starving and tired,
WE FIGHT!
Through the bullets spewing around us,
WE FIGHT!
Through the explosions, the fire, the screams,
WE FIGHT!
Through the fear, the blood, the tears,
WE FIGHT!
Though tomorrow we may not be here,
WE FIGHT!
For their life, for your life, for our lives,
WE FIGHT!
Because we're not afraid to die,
WE FIGHT!
Because we'd gladly give our lives,
WE FIGHT!
For glory's sake, for justice's sake, for freedom's sake,
WE FIGHT!
Because if we don't, who will?
WE FIGHT!

The Flag

They said "It's only a flag", as they gathered around
the red, white, and blue as it burned on the ground.
It's not just some flag, it represents more,
our history, traditions, and all Soldiers before.

It's the flag that we bear on our shoulders to war,
as we fight for our country, our freedom, and more.
It's the flag that flies high with us into the fight,
as we give our lives to protect your rights.

It's the flag that we use to cover over our dead,
when we bring them back home to the states once again.
It's the flag lifted from my friend's coffin with pride,
the flag that we gave to his wife as she cried.

It's the flag that we proudly salute as we stand,
as we think of the Soldiers who died for these lands.
It's a symbol of hope and the freedoms we have,
so don't you dare tell me "It's only a flag".

Good Ole Jodi

Dear Good Ole Jodi,

Hope this note finds you well.
I found out about you, in case you couldn't tell.

You entered my home while I was overseas,
you brought my family and life to its knees.

Countless hours of fights, endless arguments too,
and every last one revolved right around you.

But I don't blame you Jodi, no, it's not just your fault.
My wife learned it's hers, as divorce has now taught.

I live with my kids while she's broke and alone,
in that now empty house that I once called my home.

So, feel free to stop by, I'm sure you know the way,
since now she's not married, I'm sure it's ok.

Please make sure to say hi when you see her for me.
I wish you only the best, my good friend, Ole Jodi.

The Soldier's Resolve

Hear our voices roar, fear our battle cries,
a sign that foreshadows your early demise.
"Get ready to charge!" is announced once again,
so soon my dear foe you know you will be dead.
As the signal goes off, we let out our screams,
a true demonstration of what valor means.
We push through the bullets and hazes of war,
with courage like nothing that you've seen before.
Our unwavering charge, our relentless attack,
quickly pushes your defensive lines farther back.
As we break through your ranks, and our men they draw near,
your men turn and run, overwhelmed by their fear.
Though for now some escaped, you know it won't be long,
For we'll never stop 'til we've beaten you all.
'Twas your biggest mistake making us get involved,
For hell hath no fury like a Soldier's resolve.

The Count Down

"Get ready to land!" The crew chief yells from the back,
while the pilot in front screams "We're under attack!"
Ten, Nine,
as the bird drops in flight.
Eight, Seven,
I recall every lesson.
Six, Five,
fear sinks in I might die.
Four, Three,
it's either them, or it's me.
Two, One,
my war has begun.

Sitting Alone

Sitting in silence, alone with my thoughts.
I think of the wars and the lessons they taught.
I think about battles, and I think about friends.
I think of those lost, who I won't see again.

I remember the horrors, the pain, and the fear,
the death, and the sadness that was always too near.
I remember the faces of the corpses in graves,
the unforgettable stench of death and decay.

I see the face of a child, afraid and alone
because the war took her parents, along with her home.
But she was still lucky, because she's still alive,
unlike the countless other children who've died.

I hear the voice of a friend calling out for my aid
as I fight, still pinned down, as the voice starts to fade.
I remember the scene of my friend on the ground,
his body lifeless and cold, with his blood spilt around.

I recall seeing his wife for the first time back home,
as I ask for forgiveness because she's now alone.
Though it wasn't my fault, I still blame myself,
as I think of the ways that I could have helped.

I relive moments of pain from when I earned my scars.
I feel the sting and the burn from where they've left their mark.
I fall into darkness, a bottomless hole,
and this is the reason why I don't sit alone.

Fireworks

A flash and a bang, they light up the sky,
as everyone revels this fourth of July.
The crowds; they all marvel at the show up above,
as Americans celebrate this country they love.
But I sit here in silence, staring off at the blasts,
as the flash and the noise bring me back to my past.

The bangs like the blasts that would crater the ground,
tossing out shrapnel and dirt all around.
The light from the flash like explosions too near,
that swallowed my friends, who are no longer here.
As these thoughts of battle and loss fill my head,
I think of each outcome, the pain, and the dead.

While I recall these moments my heart starts to race,
my family, they notice the look on my face.
It's not one of joy, or one full of cheer,
but a face filled with anger, anxiety, and fear.

They ask me what's wrong, but they won't understand
the thoughts and the feelings only us Soldiers can.
People say that they get it, but they'll never know
the pain they can cause with a firework show.

Intrusive Thoughts (Unwanted Guest)

Who invited you, the worst of friends,
as you slowly creep into my head?
You bring with you some other guests,
like anger, pain; unwanted stress.
Like nervousness when alone in a crowd,
or the tension that builds when the noise is too loud.
The reluctance I feel when I give out my trust,
and the feelings the same if it's someone I love.

Hopeless thoughts that the world all around me is mad,
and the people within it are inherently bad.
Pondering as I ask if the world is deranged,
and telling myself that it won't ever change.

Feeling trapped, stuck inside of this rut that you hate;
though you want it to change, you think it is too late.
And with all of these thoughts swimming round in my head,
you wouldn't believe all the things that I've said.

You can try reaching out and seek a helping hand,
but unless they've been through it, they just don't understand.
Thus I'm writing these words so that someone may know,
if you're going through this, you are never alone.

You see, I know your pain and I know your fears,
Because I have lived through them for all these years.
Even though you feel lost, get those thoughts out your head!
Please believe when I say… you're not better off dead.

Alexander R. Stewart

"The Letter"

Dear loving Soldier, serving overseas,
deployment and distance has proved too hard for me.
I'm cold and I'm lonely as I lay down at night,
because you are not here to keep close and hold tight.

The distance apart and time you've been away,
has made me realize we should go separate ways.
I can no longer sit and wait idly by
for your deployment to end and you finally arrive.

For while you have been absent, I've met someone new,
and it felt only fair that I write and tell you.
When you finally come home, know that I will be gone.
Please take care of yourself, my ex-love, my dear John.

The Sentry

Another day has come and gone,
so now I sit on guard alone.
My body is tired from the day's patrol,
my bones they ache, my hands are cold.

I feel my eyes begin to shut,
and do what I must to wake back up.
"Don't Fall Asleep!" I tell myself,
for if I dream, no one will help.

For I alone stand watch tonight
and will let nothing escape my sight.
My friends trust me to do my task,
until relief arrives at last.

So here I'll stand with watchful eyes,
and if they come, they'll surely die.
For I'll allow no harm tonight
to the Soldiers who trust me as they sleep tight.

Although I'm alone, they know I will suffice.
To keep them all safe, I will sacrifice.
"Don't Fall Asleep!"

Take a Knee

Just a few miles longer, I can't let them see,
the truth that my body is quitting on me.

On a ruck, or a run, when just having some fun,
I see clearer and clearer that my times almost done.
No; it's not weakness, tiredness, or fatigue,
it's the wars that I fought taking their toll on me.

A scar from a blast, a bullet wound here,
they're causing me more pain than I ever feared.
The headaches won't go, the ringing just stays,
I keep telling myself that I will be ok.

But the truth breaks my heart, yet I know it must be,
the times coming soon when I can't just take a knee.

Behavioral Health

I know something is off, but what can I do?
If you talk about stress, they all look down on you.
They'll say that I'm weak when I am not near,
they'll laugh and they'll say that I don't belong here.

I won't get into schools without a waiver or two,
even if I am stronger or more skilled than you.
I'll get cast to the side without a second thought,
even after the hard work and things that I've taught.

But nothing has changed, I'm as sharp as I've been.
I can still fight and still push with the best of the men.
See I just need to vent, talk through thoughts in my mind,
and that is no reason to leave me here behind.

I've just been through some things as I've fought through these wars,
that resulted in issues I can't stand anymore.
Though I know my own limits, and I know I'm not well.
I won't deal with the stigma around Behavioral Health.

Incoming, Incoming, Incoming!

Incoming, Incoming, Incoming! The alarm, it loudly shrieks,
    as I jump up out of the cot and tie boots onto my feet.

While the rounds keep flying over and the ground around is struck,
    I sprint across the compound and make my way toward my truck.
      We mount the weapons into place and let the engines roar,
    while we listen on the radio for our next set of orders.

      The convoy rushes to the scene, we jump out of our doors.
Our Sergeant says to render aid to those bleeding on the floor.
We move the casualties to the truck, our Sergeant yells "Well Done!",
    then fear pours slowly into his eyes and he screams out to duck.

With flash and bangs now all around, the ground beneath us shakes.
    We realize now that we're exposed; we see our grave mistake.
    The enemy knew that we would come and so they sat and wait,
      for the reinforcements to arrive, and thus, more lives to take.

Sprawled out lying on the ground I can hear a distant humming,
      of my Sergeant yelling across the net…
        Incoming, Incoming, Incoming!

Alexander R. Stewart

Why We Drink

You say we've got a problem. You say we've had enough.
You say we've had too many and that we drink too much.

But I think that you don't get it, you just don't understand.
It's not about us getting drunk, there's more to it my friend.

We drink so we remember, we drink so we forget.
We drink for all the good times and the things that we regret.

We drink for all the fallen, we drink 'cause we're still here.
So pour a glass, I'll raise a toast and pass another beer!

Broken Switch

The war is over and done, and I'm finally back home.
So why do I still feel on edge whenever I'm alone?
I lock every door and check every place,
even though I'm at home and I know that I'm safe.
But it doesn't stop there, oh no, there's much more,
it makes it hard to enjoy the things I did before.
People put me on edge until they've earned my trust,
which is something that now isn't easily won.
I can't even enjoy a day out in a crowd,
there's just too many people; the noise is too loud.
I can't help but feel anxious, can't help but feel stressed,
I'm told "try to stay calm" and I give it my best.
I can't go out for dinner without watching the doors,
and I stare at the people as they walk 'cross the floor.
When I'm trying to sleep and I hear a strange sound,
I jump out of my bed and I check all around.
Now I can't fall asleep without weapons nearby,
I've now grown too used to my gun at my side.
Living this way steals my comfort and joy.
It's distressing; I'm starting to get more annoyed.
There's no reason to be this on edge anymore,
it's frustrating that I'm not the same as before.
I'm no longer at war and I want this to stop.
So can someone please help me? I can't turn it off!

About the Author

Sergeant First Class Alexander R. Stewart is an active-duty Soldier from Warwick, NY. He's a decorated and multi-talented human, holding membership in the Armor Association's Order of Saint George, the National Society of Leadership and Success, as well as Phi Theta Kappa Honor Society. Amid his career, he has fought three combat tours which included serving in Afghanistan, Iraq, and Syria.

Currently stationed at Fort Moore, GA as a Drill Instructor, SFC Stewart lives with his wonderful wife and two beautiful children. When he's not writing poetry, he enjoys playing music, spending time outdoors, boxing, or bettering himself through education.

www.ingramcontent.com/pod-product-compliance
Lightning Source LLC
LaVergne TN
LVHW092101060526
838201LV00047B/1500